Incredibly Insane Sports

BMX

By Jessica Cohn

Gareth Stevens
Publishing

Please visit our website, www.garethstevens.com. For a free color catalog of all our high-quality books, call toll free 1-800-542-2595 or fax 1-877-542-2596.

Library of Congress Cataloging-in-Publication Data

Cohn, Jessica.
BMX / Jessica Cohn.
     p. cm.   (Incredibly insane sports)
Includes index.
ISBN 978-1-4339-8823-3 (pbk.)
ISBN 978-1-4339-8824-0 (6-pack)
ISBN 978-1-4339-8822-6 (library binding)
1. Bicycle motocross--Juvenile literature. I. Title.
GV1049.3.C64 2013
796.6'22—dc23

2012023553

First Edition
Published in 2013 by
Gareth Stevens Publishing
111 East 14th Street, Suite 349
New York, NY 10003

©2013 Gareth Stevens Publishing

Produced by Netscribes Inc.
Art Director Dibakar Acharjee
Editorial Content The Wordbench
Copy Editor Sarah Chassé
Picture Researcher Sandeep Kumar G
Designer Rishi Raj
Illustrators Ashish Tanwar, Indranil Ganguly, Prithwiraj Samat, and Rohit Sharma

Photo credits:
Page no. = #, t = top, a = above, b = below, l = left, r = right, c = center
Front Cover: Shutterstock Images LLC Title Page: Shutterstock Images LLC
Contents Page: Shutterstock Images LLC Inside: Netscribes Inc.: 9b, 13t Shutterstock Images LLC: 4, 5, 6, 7t, 7b, 8, 9t, 10, 11, 12, 13c, 13b, 14, 15, 16, 17t, 17b, 18, 19t, 19b, 20, 21t, 21b, 22t, 22b, 23t, 23b, 24, 26, 27, 28, 29, 30, 31t, 31b, 33b, 34, 35t, 35b, 36t, 36b, 37, 38, 39t, 39b, 40, 41, 42, 43.

Printed in the United States of America

CPSIA compliance information: Batch #CW13GS: For further information contact Gareth Stevens, New York, New York at 1-800-542-2595.

Contents

RAMPED UP

To ride on a BMX monster ramp, a racer must move fast. **Freestyle** racers speed so quickly, they fly without wings. The racers perform dangerous rolls and flips in a matter of seconds. They twist in the air, spinning their bikes beneath them. Only the stars of BMX are up to the challenge. They train thousands of hours to prepare for these amazing feats.

BMX stands for "Bicycle Motocross." The X stands in as a sign for the word "cross." Motocross is a kind of motorcycle racing.

On Track

The ramps used for special events often start with a giant slide, called a roll-in, followed by a gap that the rider must fly over. The racer can roll 40 miles per hour and faster during the course of the race. The final section of the mega ramps often features a quarter pipe, which is a ramp that looks like the inside of a pipe cut in fourths. Smaller quarter pipes can be found in BMX parks around the country.

At local BMX parks, riders learn to navigate the quarter pipe. Riders start by approaching the low part of the ramp, and then they build their way up.

X Marks the Sport

Freestyle tricks are just one exciting aspect of BMX. To test a rider's strength and speed, there is also track racing, where the racers have to get around the other bikes and riders. There is nothing tame about this breakout sport. The racers practice on dirt roads, beaches, and other rough **terrain**. They race in all kinds of weather.

Each BMX racecourse presents a different set of challenges, but they all are built for speed.

Staying on Track

More than 370 different BMX tracks have been built in the United States. Yet they all share certain features. They have starting gates and a series of straightaways and turns. The riders gain speed on the flat and straight parts of the track. They use their muscle power to fight against **gravity**.

Dirt competitions are held on tracks made from sand that has been pressed into fine pieces.

TEST IT!

Anything you can touch is made of matter, and matter has gravity, which pulls on matter around it. Bigger things have more gravity, which is why Earth has more pull than anything else around. To study Earth's gravitational strength, try spinning a hoop on your hips. The movement creates a force that holds the hoop up. But at some point, you stop spinning the hoop, and Earth's gravity pulls the hoop down.

STARTING LINE

It all began in California. Many people trace the start of BMX to the summer of 1969 and a Los Angeles park, where a group of boys wanted to race their bikes. There was a teen working there who knew about motorcycle racing, and he helped the younger racers get organized.

Before racing at an event, successful racers study the track. They watch other people go around the track to see what happens.

Meet Up

That first summer, the bikers raced on Thursday nights for 10 weeks in a row, and the winners each won a **trophy**. Before long, the excitement was spreading. In Southern California, it is possible to ride bikes all year long. The area is known for its sunshine and lack of rain, and in these conditions the sport grew fast. Now, BMX tracks, clubs, and larger associations can be found across the country.

TEST IT!

Grab a pencil, a ruler, and paper and try to draw a plan for a track. There is no rule about the number of hills, but there are some requirements.

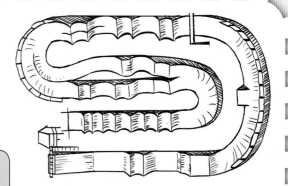

Requirements for a BMX Track
Gate: at least 24 feet wide
First straightaway: 25 to 35 feet wide
Track after first turn: 15 to 20 feet wide
Total track: 900 to 1,200 feet long

If 1 inch equals 20 feet, how long does your track have to be from start to finish?

Answer: The shortest track is 900 feet, and 900 divided by 20 is 45, so it must be at least 45 inches on paper.

Old School

The first official BMX races were held in the 1970s. The early **sprints** were action-packed, and the riders could do awesome tricks. But in the 1980s, people turned more of their attention to freestyle cycling. The freestyle riders were especially flashy. In the 1990s, BMX became more popular again. By then, the racers were adding more freestyle moves to their performances.

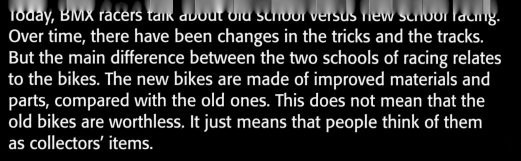

Today, BMX racers talk about old school versus new school racing. Over time, there have been changes in the tricks and the tracks. But the main difference between the two schools of racing relates to the bikes. The new bikes are made of improved materials and parts, compared with the old ones. This does not mean that the old bikes are worthless. It just means that people think of them as collectors' items.

Riders who can balance with both feet on the pedals at the starting gate are able to start off faster than the others.

WHEELS OF TIME

O f all sports, BMX is one of the youngest. Bicycles were invented before motorcycles. The first two-wheeled bikes appeared in the early 1800s, and the motorcycle was first introduced in the late 1800s. But BMX racing did not begin until after the start of motorcycle racing.

The first bike tires were iron bands wrapped around wooden wheels. In the mid-1880s, some tires were made of leather around an air-filled rubber tube, but they were costly. In the late 1800s, an affordable air-filled rubber tire was introduced.

History in the Making

1885 A German engineer named Gottlieb Daimler introduced the gas-powered motorcycle.

early 1900s Racers in the United Kingdom held motorcycle trials. These races were known as scrambles and then motocross.

1957 The first world championship for motocross was held.

1970s Bike racers adopted the rules of motocross to create BMX racing.

2008 BMX racing became an Olympic sport.

Motocross became a sport before BMX racing, but both were introduced to the Olympics in the same year.

Making the Jump

Today's young riders punish the pavement, putting in practice time to master the sport. Skilled racers make heart-stopping double jumps. They can ride up one ramp, fly through the air, and land on another ramp, facing downward. The most famous BMX riders can make a big show of getting to the finish line. On the way, they grab **big air**.

Public skateparks have been built for skating, skateboarding, and BMX. The first skatepark was built in California in 1976.

Safe Speeds

The racers travel at high speeds. Yet BMX is considered one of the safest action sports. That is because racers go through a lot of practice to get to the top. The record of injuries is low, when compared with other extreme sports.

BMX officials are serious about their jobs. They check the equipment carefully. They make sure people follow the rules.

In places where there are no public skateparks, racers often set up their own courses and even construct their own ramps.

FULLY EQUIPPED

The bikes used in BMX come in two main sizes: 20 inches (51 cm) or 24 inches (61 cm). These numbers tell the **diameter** of the wheels. The bikes are also measured from the seat to the handlebars, along the top tube. The taller the rider, the longer the tube should be. It is important to get a bike that fits.

Machine Made

All bikes include **simple machines**, such as wheels and **axles**, that work together. But the parts of a BMX bike are unique in important ways. For example, BMX bikes have only one speed. The rear gear stays the same no matter what.

Shocking!

In a regular bike, the suspension is the system that protects the rider from the effects of riding over rough ground. When a rider goes over a bump, several moving parts around the tires and seat take in the shock. This lessens the shock to the rider. But classic BMX bikes have no suspension. The rider has to power through any bumps in the road.

The 20- or 24-inch wheels of a BMX bike are several inches smaller than those of other kinds of bikes.

Getting Fit

General guidelines for a bike's fit are listed, but to get the right fit for a BMX bike, it is best to go to a bike shop.

age	height in inches	tube in inches
4 to 7	40 to 48	16 to 17
7 to 9	48 to 54	16 to 18
8 to 11	50 to 57	18 to 19
10 to 12	54 to 60	19 to 20
11 to 13	56 to 64	20
13 to 16	60 to 72	20.5
16 and over	65 to 72	21
tall adults	72 and above	21.5

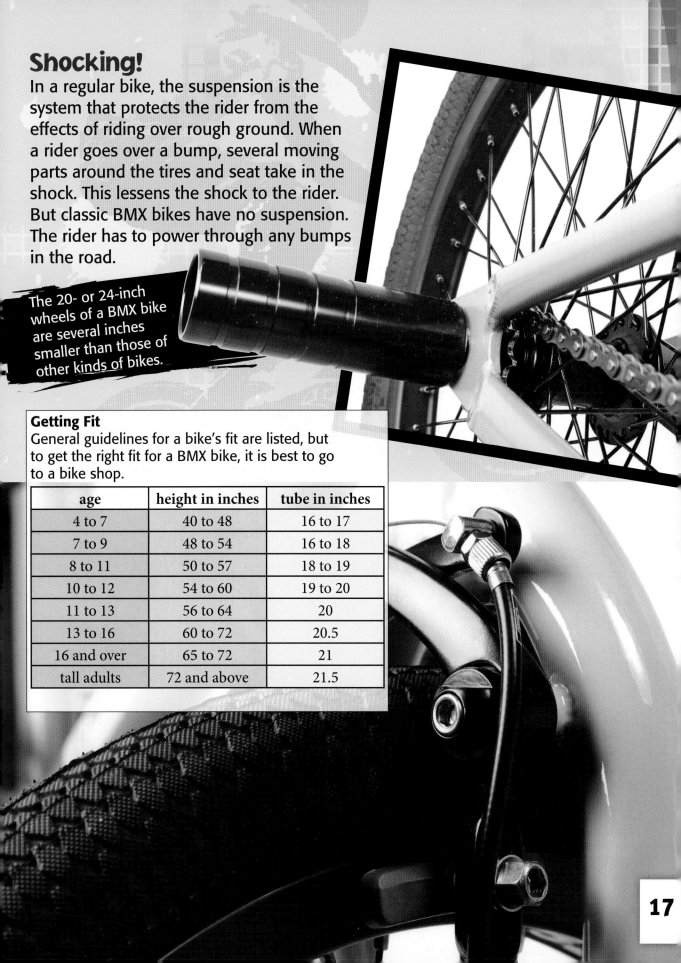

Tech Talk

This ride is a rush. The basics of BMX have not changed since the sport began. There is a rider, a bike, and a track, and the rider is trying to beat a record. Since the 1970s, however, the equipment has been improved. New materials make the bikes stronger, and people have been studying how to make the parts of the bikes work better. For example, the metal rims inside the tires have been made to bend so they are less likely to pop the tires. Pedals have been shaped for easier footing.

The shape of the bike frame, with triangles in the front and back, supports the rider and the rider's movements.

Data Driven

Some of the newest bikes have parts that measure the bike's movement. On the hub of the wheel, they have **cogs** loaded with high-tech parts that can keep track of the bike's movements and send this information to a computer. The computer reads the bike's speed and **velocity**. It can even measure how much the rider moves from side to side. This information can be used to show the rider how to improve his or her movements.

hub

Successful riders get a feel for the forces that affect their bikes.

TEST IT!

Velocity is the speed a bike goes in one direction. The bike's direction is always changing somewhat. So velocity is measured as the rate at which the bike changes its position. When the bike turns a corner, the velocity changes. See for yourself by riding a bike or skateboard and paying attention to how it feels to turn a corner.

19

WEAR AND TEAR

The newest safety gear helps riders avoid injuries. Pads cover elbows and knees. Special protectors are worn over the chest and shins. The most important item is a helmet to protect the head. The newest full-face helmets also cover the ears.

full-face helmet

elbow guards

gloves

knee pads

The new helmets have stickers that show they are certified as safe. For racing, the helmet should have an ASTM International sticker. ASTM stands for American Society for Testing and Materials.

Got You Covered

Experienced riders keep their legs covered. Long sleeves protect the arms. This is not a sport for flip-flops or bare feet. Riders need to cover their feet and wear socks that cover their ankles as well.

Helmets prevent brain injury. The helmet should fit correctly. It should not be too loose or too tight.

Time on the Bike

To win, riders must practice every chance they can get. The stars of BMX racing take every opportunity to ride their bikes. They may also put in time at a gym, to help build their muscles. However, it's the actual riding that trains people to win racing competitions. The key to success in this sport is **conditioning**. In BMX, conditioning does not just build muscles. It exercises the heart and other organs and even trains the mind.

Besides time on a bike, the most important thing is fueling the body with healthful foods. The body also needs water to work well.

Going Pro

All BMX **professionals** started by learning to ride a bike. Then, they put in the time needed to master it. It takes thousands of hours to become a world-class racer. There are no shortcuts that a racer can take to get to the top.

The bikes come in three kinds. They are jump or dirt bikes, racing bikes, and freestyle or stunt bikes.

PATH TO THE TOP

The riders sign up for races based on the size of their bikes. A rider with a 20-inch (51 cm) bike is grouped with people with the same size bike. That group is further divided by age and experience. A rookie is someone who is new. The next level is **novice**. The levels that follow are expert, **elite** master, "B" pro, and "A" pro.

In BMX, men and women compete in separate races.

The X Games are yearly contests run by ESPN, a cable TV network.

Moving On

A BMX rider can advance from one level to the next level by placing first and winning points. A novice is considered ready after winning enough races to move on. The higher the rider goes, the more points he or she gets for a first-place win.

What Do You Think?

Many BMX riders welcome the chance to share their sport with TV audiences. Think about the sports you have seen on TV. How are these sports also like businesses?

25

Events of the Day

A moto is a **qualifying** race. It's intense! Winners of the motos race one another in finals called the mains. At large gatherings, they have to hold semi mains first, because there are so many people. Then the winners of the semi mains go on to the mains.

An open is a race where points are not awarded. The opens give racers a chance to go up against people with better records. Losing will not hurt them much, because points will not be taken away. The opens are more like shows than races.

The races happen in a single lap, or one time around the track. The course is groomed so there is nothing to trip up the racers.

Three Chances

Usually, enough people show up to make it possible for everyone to have several chances to qualify for the mains. At the motos, a racer usually ends up racing several times with the people in his or her group. At the end of the day, the racers within each group are ranked. Those on top can go on to the mains, or finals. In the mains, the racers compete against people in their age-group.

POINTS WELL TAKEN

Amateurs race to win points and trophies. Professionals can collect prize money in addition to other awards. There are two ways of judging the riders. Which one sounds better to you?

Moto System

In this kind of racing, each racer competes in every round. Each time he or she is scored against all the people in the same class. The higher the total points, the more likely it is that the person will advance to the mains. This is called cumulative scoring.

Pros
This kind of scoring rewards racers who put in a strong showing each time. It rewards people who are consistent.

Cons
The points are awarded in a somewhat complicated way. Sometimes, mistakes can be made.

Transfer System

Instead of getting points, the racers simply try to cross the finish line ahead of the others. Once someone wins a round, he or she sits out until the final races. At the mains, the top finishers meet and compete again.

Pros
Most people get more than one chance to advance. So someone who was "off" during the first race has a chance to perform better the next time.

Cons
People can win just because someone else made a mistake. In addition, the early winners do not get to race much because they must sit out until the mains.

During a day of racing, people compete against other people in their class. The classes are decided by the size of the racer's bike and other factors, such as how long the racer has been competing.

DIFFERENT LEAGUES

As in any sport, the BMX athletes compete in a league. The American Bicycle Association was started in 1977. It became known as the ABA. The National Bicycle League was started in Miami, Florida, in 1974. It was known as the NBL. The leagues welcomed new members and worked to provide a safe place for young riders to ride and learn.

Joining the Clubs

In 2011, the ABA and the NBL joined together. The agreement makes it possible for members of either group to race at any track. Both the NBL and the ABA have started calling themselves USA BMX.

Skills Testing

At local BMX clubs, new riders can work on their skills and learn from others. It is one thing to read about popping a wheelie. It is another thing to be at a club, watching someone perform one. The rider moves his or her weight to the back of the bike and leans forward while pulling at the handlebars.

TEST IT!

The center of gravity is the center of an object's mass. To test this idea, try cutting out odd cardboard shapes. Guess their centers of gravity, and then try balancing the shapes on the eraser of a pencil.

On a person, the center of gravity is near the belly button. To force the front wheel of a bike up, the rider must move his or her center back on the bike.

Going for Gold

BMX racing can be fun to watch and even more thrilling to do. This sport has long attracted top athletes. But when BMX events were added to the Summer Olympic Games, even more people became excited about cycling. After the United States sent racers to the Olympics in 2008, cycling clubs began to notice increased interest in the sport.

BMX is viewed as an American invention with worldwide appeal. The sport made its second Olympic showing in 2012, at the Summer Games in London, England.

Team USA

The people who **sanction** BMX events at the Olympics are part of an international group. It is called the International Cycling Union. In sports, certain groups control the events and the rules. It is the International Cycling Union that decides who gets to compete in BMX events at the games. Its members keep track of the riders' rankings.

A special track was built for the 2012 Olympics in London. After the games, it was opened to the public.

RACE TO FAME

Olympic athletes are joining established stars of the sport, such as Ryan Nyquist. He has won many championships in dirt jumping and other events. The stars also include pioneers of the sport, such as Stu Thomsen, who raced in the 1970s and 1980s. He became a professional racer at age 16. Thomsen was so successful, he was called "The Man."

Ryan Nyquist has been winning awards for more than 10 years.

Fast and Famous

Today's stars and legends are inspiring new riders to take up the sport. In fact, many BMX stars take an active role in encouraging the new riders. They act as teachers by making how-to videos that show the tailwhip, the barspin, and other tricks.

In a tailwhip, the back of the bike spins around the front end, while the rider seems to hang in the air. In a barspin, the rider spins the bars, either halfway or all the way around. The barspin is one of the tricks that made Ryan Nyquist famous.

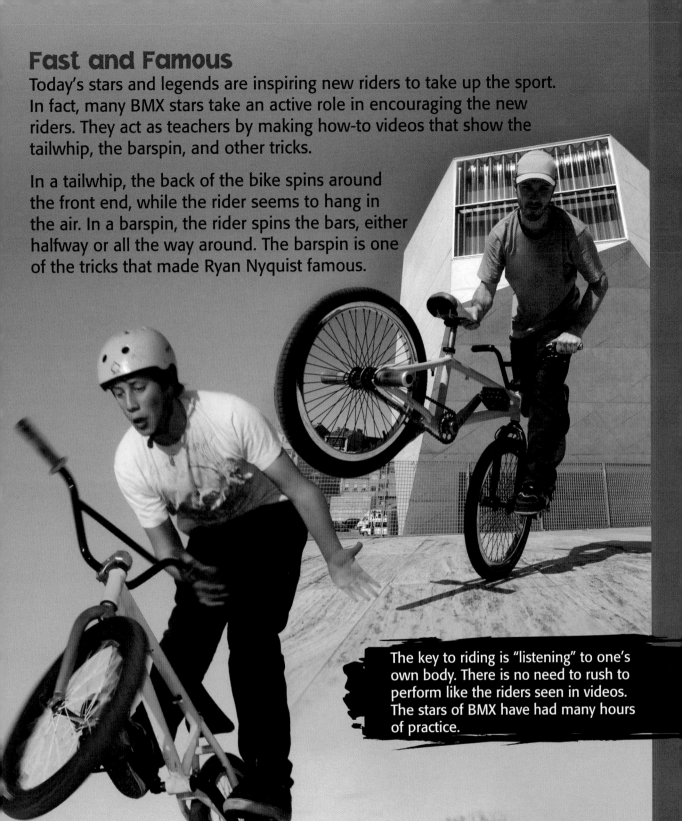

The key to riding is "listening" to one's own body. There is no need to rush to perform like the riders seen in videos. The stars of BMX have had many hours of practice.

Star Power

BMX champions and stunt riders have learned to use their star power to send positive messages. Stunt riders such as Matt Wilhelm visit schools across the country to talk about things they believe in. Wilhelm became known to the public when he appeared on the TV show *America's Got Talent*. Now, he puts on shows at schools, where he talks about the importance of having good character.

Stunt riders often help important causes, such as efforts to stop bullying in schools.

Right Kind of Ride

Riders of all ranks know that the excitement of the sport can be used to help others. For example, the BMX Race For Life events raise money to help people with illnesses. BMX teams across the nation organize rides to help charities. People give bikes and bike parts to people who might not have them otherwise.

Racers have organized many events to teach young people about bike safety.

READY TO RIDE

Can you picture yourself as a BMX racer? Are you ready to ramp up your exercise? Many families participate as a family activity. They join associations such as USA BMX. This allows them to practice at tracks that are approved by the association. It also lets the athletes compete at the group's events.

Road Forward

The best way to start is to get going. Take bike rides to build strength. If you cannot reach an official track, ride elsewhere. Look for pavement with no traffic. Find paved areas that are blocked off, and make sure it is OK to ride there. Always wear a helmet. Go your own speed to see where it takes you.

TEST IT!

New riders need to get a feel not only for speed, but for inertia. This is the way an object, such as a bike, resists starting or stopping. Consider this law of motion: An object at rest tends to remain at rest, and an object in motion tends to remain in motion. Now, think about a truck and a bike rolling downhill with no brakes. Which one is harder to stop?

Answer: Greater mass tends to mean greater inertia, so the truck is harder to stop.

To learn to ride a bike, start by getting a feel for balance. Start by coasting and gliding. Then, try to pedal.

See Where It Goes

Bikes are sold at yard sales and resale shops, so a new rider does not need expensive equipment. Just make sure the bike is in good condition. It is also important to get and wear the safety gear, especially the helmet.

Many clubs offer trial memberships, which do not cost as much as full memberships. Just going to the races is usually free, and everyone is welcome.

Many bike shops offer a safety check of secondhand equipment. Bike shop professionals can also help new riders find a helmet that fits.

It's Huge

In the world of BMX, the races are happening all year long. The first thing to do is become skilled at bike riding, and for that a rider needs to go for a spin as often as possible.

Find out what the local laws are for bike riding. Look for safe places to practice.

Ride on!

41

WATCH YOUR LANGUAGE

The word "session" means "a meeting" or "the time spent on something." In BMX racing, putting in practice time is very important. So BMX racers use *session* as an action word. A rider may session from 1 to 4 in the afternoon.

When it comes to biking, most people use the word *riding* to mean "moving along on a vehicle." In the BMX world, it also means "performing."

The Word

BMX racing has a special language, though it does share some words with other extreme sports. A grind, for example, is what happens when a part of the bike is up against something and the bike slides. A half-pipe is a ramp that looks like a tube cut in half.

Words in Context
Can you guess the meaning of these BMX words and phrases?

1. Look out for the *alligator pit*. The rain on Wednesday really did a number on the track.

   alligator pit: a gap in a track that could be dangerous

2. No, he's not here today. That *butcher's* bike is in the shop.

   butcher: someone who often breaks the equipment

3. Look at that! That's what I call a *dialed* finish!

   dialed: perfect; well done

LEGENDS OF BMX

The legends of BMX are men and women whose skills and daring won attention and awards. Some were pioneers of the sport, and others were record breakers. In many cases, they have used their stardom to help others.

Five Famous Racers

In 1975, **David Clinton** was the first to win the U.S. title awarded by the National Bicycle Association.

In 1989, **Cheri Elliott** was the first female inducted into the American Bicycle Association's BMX Hall of Fame.

The Olympics featured BMX for the first time in 2008, and **Mike Day** became the highest-ranking American after winning a silver medal.

Kevin Robinson jumped 54 feet (16.5 m) high from a BMX ramp in 2008. At the time of his record-breaking jump, this American held seven X Games medals, including three gold.

On May 28, 2011, New Zealand's **Jed Mildon** performed a triple backflip, the Most Backflips on a Bicycle, according to Guinness World Records.

Behind the Legends

Each year, the National BMX Hall of Fame gives out honors in five categories, including Pioneer, Racer, and Freestyler. Here are three of the people who recently joined those ranks.

name	nickname	category	wins and accomplishments
John Palfreyman, Jr.	Snaggletooth	Pioneer	won Northern California Yamaha Gold Cup Expert Class '74, raced in world's first BMX pro race, was an original test rider for Redline Bicycles
Eric Carter	EC	Racer	won ABA #1 Amateur '86, IBMXF world titles '85, '86, '87, '88, went on to win titles in mountain biking, too
Mat Hoffman	The Condor	Freestyler	organized the X Games, president of Hoffman Bikes

Elite Class

Would you like to join the elite class of BMX experts? To start, use your library, and the Internet, to research these winners. Then, look up other years and legends.

1985	2000
David Clinton	Ronnie Anderson
Linn Kastan	Thom Lund
John George	Chuck Hooper
1990	2005
Scot Breithaupt	Greg Esser
Jeff Bottema	Yvonne Shoup
Greg Hill	Clint Miller
1995	2010
Gene Roden	Tim Judge
Bob Hadley	Steve Veltman
Jeff Kosmala	Craig "gOrk" Barrette
Pete Kelley	Woody Itson
	Linda Dorsey
	Al Fritz

Glossary

amateurs: in sports, the unpaid athletes

axles: rods on which a wheel turns

big air: great height on a jump in extreme sports

cogs: teeth on one part that fit with teeth on another part so that when the first teeth are forced to turn they create movement by engaging the second part

conditioning: training needed to be physically fit

diameter: length of a straight line across the center of a circle

elite: ruling; belonging to a group of people considered superior in some way

freestyle: allowing any trick or move from a somewhat standard set of tricks or moves

gravity: attraction between objects that have mass

novice: new to field

professionals: in sports, the athletes who are paid or sponsored

qualifying: declaring ready; measuring readiness

sanction: approve; judge as worthy

simple machines: elements, such as wheels and axles, used to make complex machines

sprints: short races at top speeds

terrain: features of land or of an area

trophy: a symbolic award earned through a victory

velocity: the speed of something traveling in a given direction

For More Information

Books

Ciencin, Scott. *BMX Blitz.* Mankato, MN: Stone Arch Books, 2011.

Donaldson, Tony. *BMX Trix & Techniques for the Park & Street.* Osceola, WI: MBI, 2004.

Intercity, Gavin Lucas, and Stuart Robinson. *Rad Rides: The Best BMX Bikes of All Time.* London, UK: Laurence King Publishers, 2012.

Kelley, K.C. *Stunt Bicycle Riding.* Milwaukee, WI: Gareth Stevens, 2003.

DVD

Dave Mirra's Trick Tips, Vol. 1: BMX Basics. Dave Mirra and others. (2001)

Websites

The Exploratorium's Science of Cycling
www.exploratorium.edu/cycling/
The Exploratorium is part of the Science Learning Network, supported by the Franklin Institute, and "Science of Cycling" explains how bikes work.

USA BMX: The American Bicycle Association
www.usabmx.com
The former NBL and ABA combine efforts at the new USA BMX website, which offers up-to-the-minute news on events, riders, and rankings.

Index